SPELL CHECKERS™

VOLUME 3

An Oni Press Publication

SPELL CHECKERS™

VOLUME 3: CARELESS WHISPER

written by
JAMIE S. RICH

illustrated by
NICOLAS HITORI DE

flashbacks and cover
illustrated by
JOËLLE JONES

cover colored by
WARREN WUCINICH

lettered by
WARREN WUCINICH

designed by
KEITH A. WOOD

edited by
JILL BEATON

Oni Press, Inc.

PUBLISHER, JOE NOZEMACK

EDITOR IN CHIEF, JAMES LUCAS JONES

ART DIRECTOR, KEITH WOOD

DIRECTOR OF PUBLICITY, JOHN SCHORK

DIRECTOR OF SALES, CHEYENNE ALLOTT

EDITOR, JILL BEATON

EDITOR, CHARLIE CHU

GRAPHIC DESIGNER, JASON STOREY

DIGITAL PREPRESS LEAD, TROY LOOK

ADMINISTRATIVE ASSISTANT, ROBIN HERRERA

Oni Press Inc.
1305 SE Martin Luther King Jr. Blvd.
Suite A
Portland, OR 97214

WWW.ONIPRESS.COM

First Edition: October 2013

ISBN: 978-1-62010-094-3
eISBN: 978-1-62010-107-0
Library of Congress Control Number: 2013937932

1 3 5 7 9 10 8 6 4 2

Printed in the U.S.A.

Chapter I
"Say You'll Go"

I

13

...MONARCHISM IS AN OUTMODED SYSTEM ONLY LAMENTED BY NERDS AND THE INTELLECTUALLY LAZY.

SERIOUSLY, SO MUCH VIRGINITY IS GOING TO BE LOST TONIGHT, I'M NOT SURE THERE'LL BE ANY LEFT.

FIRST UP, THE FOUR LUCKY DUDES WHO WOULD BE KING.

JIMMY WOLFE. NO SURPRISE THERE, HE LETTERED IN THREE DIFFERENT SPORTS.

AND YET HE CAN'T SPELL HIS OWN NAME. IT'S TWO LETTERS TOO LONG.

IT'S A FAMILY AFFAIR. *KYLE AND DEREK HERNANDEZ.*

A GENE POOL INBRED ENOUGH, THEY MIGHT AS WELL BE ROYALTY.

AND LAST, BUT NOT LEAST, A SURPRISE...

MARLON SPRINGFIELD!

OH, HEAVENLY DOG!

OKAY, LET'S MEET THE LADIES IN WAITING...

PATTY HOPPER!

PANTY DROPPER!

JILLY BEATDOWN!

SEE WHAT HAPPENS WHEN THE JUGGALOS ALL VOTE AS ONE?

CLAUDINE CHEVALIER!

GIDDY-UP! STABLEHANDS NEED LOVE, TOO!

AND ROUNDING OUT OUR SELECTION OF PRETTY PRINCESSES...

GAG! I BET IT'S ANOTHER...

16

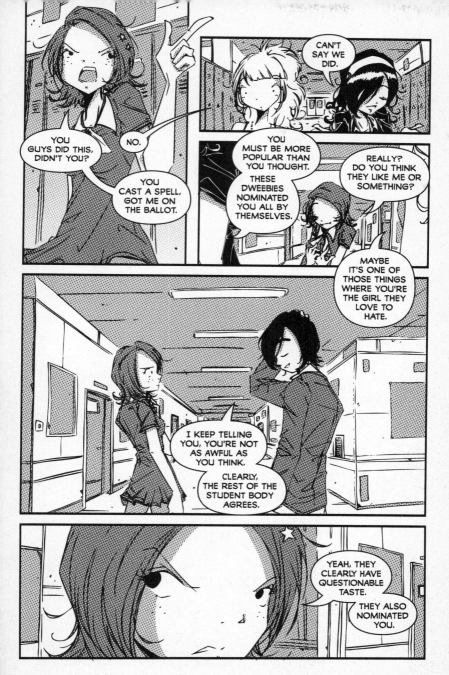

BUT YOU *DO* WANT TO WIN?

YES, JESSE.

YOU JUST DON'T WANT US TO RIG IT?

EXACTLY.

RIIIIIGHT. I HEAR YA.

YOU "FORBID" US FROM USING MAGIC. YOU "WON" THIS "YOURSELF."

NO, YOU NUMBSKULL. I REALLY MEAN IT.

NO WITCHY HELP. I EITHER WIN THIS, OR I DON'T.

I DON'T GET IT. WHAT'S THE ANGLE?

THERE IS NO ANGLE.

I JUST... I ALWAYS WANTED TO BE A PRINCESS. IF IT'S GOING TO HAPPEN, I WANT IT TO BE REAL.

EITHER OF YOU LAUGHS, AND YOU'LL BE FIRST AGAINST THE WALL!

ARE WE CLEAR?

YES, YOUR MAJESTY!

NO MAGIC!

VERY GOOD. AS YOU WERE.

SO, WAIT, WAS SHE REALLY SERIOUS?

OR IS THIS SOME KIND OF REVERSE PSYCHIATRY THING?

YOU MEAN LIKE TELLING US NOT TO CAST A SPELL AS A WAY TO MAKE SURE WE ACTUALLY DO?

I DON'T KNOW, KIMMIE. MAYBE.

IT'S PROBABLY SAFER JUST TO DO WHAT SHE SAYS, THOUGH.

I GUESS.

SAY, HAS ANYONE ASKED YOU TO BE THEIR DATE?

NOPE. NO ONE.

23

DID YOU GUYS GO FULL "BIBBITY BOBBITY BOO" ALL OVER SOMETHING?

YOU KNOW IT. ONCE UPON A TIME THIS WAS A SHOEBOX WITH THREAD SPINDLES FOR WHEELS.

AND THE DRIVER IS MY MAGIC TOTEM.

JUST A SMALL ANIMATION SPELL, AND VOILA.

YOU WITCHES ARE MAGNIF'.

LET ME FINISH GETTING READY, AND I'LL BE RIGHT DOWN.

YOU GOTTA BE KIDDING ME. WE MAKE A WHOLE DAMN CAR, AND SHE ISN'T EVEN DRESSED?

THINK ABOUT IT...

...IT TAKES WAY MORE MAGIC TO MAKE THAT GIRL LOOK GOOD.

TRUE. WE HAD A WHOLE SHOEBOX TO BUILD FROM, AND SHE JUST HAS THE FACE SHE WAS BORN WITH.

I JUST HOPE WE HAVE ENOUGH JUICE...

...TO KEEP THIS THING RUNNING ALL NIGHT.

I MEAN, IT COULD TAKE EVERYTHING WE'VE GOT...

HURRY UP, POLLY.

AND MAKE SURE YOU TAKE CARE OF THAT. I DON'T WANT IT GETTING ALL FILTHY.

YEAH, POLLY, STAY CLOSE.

LIKE, DON'T CRAMP OUR STYLE OR NOTHIN', BUT BE ALERT IN CASE WE NEED SOMETHING.

YOU GIRLS, YOU SPOIL ME. YOU'VE THOUGHT OF EVERYTHING.

OH, WE'RE NOT DONE YET.

LOOK TO YOUR LEFT.

WHY DO YOU WANT ME TO LOOK AT THAT JACKASS?

NOT *HIM*.

ABOVE HIM.

ACCEPT CYNTHIA AS YOUR QUEEN

Chapter 2
"Jesse, Are You Listening?"

2

Visit Minkus at minkusgavein.tumblr.com
or on Twitter @minkus.

Visit Noémie Allard and Virgin Princesse at
https://www.facebook.com/pages/Virgin-Princesse/8606479651

40

MY MUSKY ODOR MIGHT DRAW OUT WHATEVER VERMIN LIVE UNDER THIS GYM.

SLRP

I CAN VAGUELY TASTE THAT THERE WAS PUNCH IN THERE ONCE...

SOMEONE SPIKED IT HARDER THAN AN IMMIGRANT BUILDING A RAILROAD.

YEARGH!

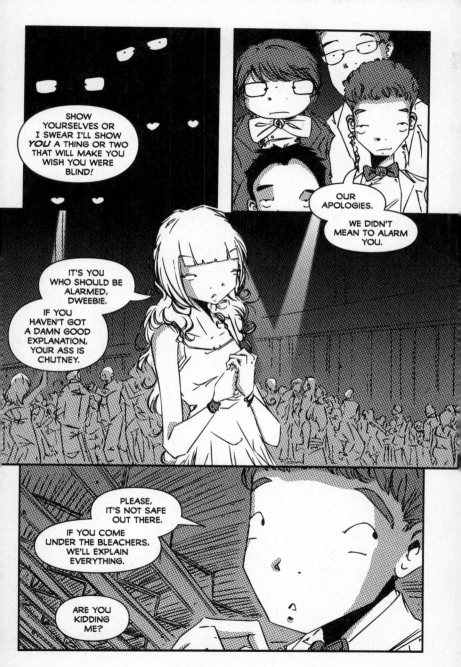

43

SHEESH! *FINE!*

THIS COULD GET ME MURDERED, BUT YOU GUYS LOOK SO PATHETIC, I SOMEHOW DOUBT IT.

THANK YOU. *HI.* MY NAME IS JED.

YOU HAVE MY WORD, WE WOULD NEVER STARE AT YOU, AT LEAST NOT IN ANY PERVERTED WAY.

GOLLY, YOU SURE KNOW HOW TO FLATTER A GIRL.

HOW MANY OF YOU IS IN THIS LITTLE CHESS CLUB, ANYWAY?

"WE ARE BUT EIGHT SCORE YOUNG BLONDES AND BRUNETTES, ALL BETWEEN SIXTEEN AND NINETEEN-AND-A-HALF, CUT OFF IN THIS CASTLE WITH NO ONE TO PROTECT US."

HUR HUR

SNICKER

HE KNOWS I WILL HIT HIM, RIGHT?

NO, NO, DON'T!

GEORGE DIDN'T MEAN ANYTHING BY IT.

RATHER, YOU SEE, THIS IS OUR PROBLEM.

WE'RE NERDS. SOCIALLY AWKWARD NERDS. WE QUOTE MONTY PYTHON AND DO OTHER NERDY THINGS...

...AND THAT'S WHY WE'RE HIDING OUT UNDER THE BLEACHERS INSTEAD OF DANCING WITH GIRLS.

YOU'RE GIVING THE SKANKS AT THIS SCHOOL WAY TOO MUCH CREDIT FOR BEING PICKY.

MAYBE, BUT YOU HEARD HOW FAST GEORGE THERE MESSED UP WITH YOU. THAT'S WHAT HAPPENS ANY TIME WE TRY TO TALK TO LADIES.

THAT'S IF WE EVEN GET CLOSE. MORE LIKELY, IF WE STEP OUT AND SHOW OUR FACES, THE JOCKS AND BULLIES WILL BEAT US TO A PULP.

WELL, YOU'RE TALKING TO ME JUST FINE. GEORGE HERE NOTWITHSTANDING.

I'M SORRY, BUT NO. THIS IS STUPID.

THERE AREN'T ENOUGH DISCO BEATS ON THE PLANET TO MAKE CHESS CLUB LOOK COO--

FINE.

I AM SURE I WILL REGRET THIS.

COME ON, GRAND MOFF NERDKIN, LET'S SHAKE SOME LEGS.

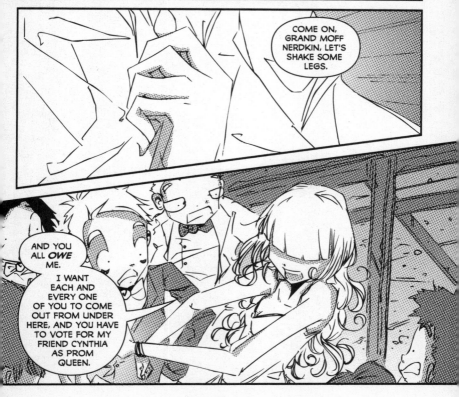

AND YOU ALL *OWE* ME.

I WANT EACH AND EVERY ONE OF YOU TO COME OUT FROM UNDER HERE, AND YOU HAVE TO VOTE FOR MY FRIEND CYNTHIA AS PROM QUEEN.

WAIT HERE, DWEEBIE.

I'LL BE BACK.

WHAT'S UP, BUTTERCUP?

YOU BEEN HANDING OUT FREE SAMPLES OF YOUR PSYCHOCANDY AGAIN?

HAR HAR.

YOU MAY SCOFF, BUT I'VE TAKEN ON A LITTLE PROJECT.

THANKS TO SOME DANCEFLOOR GERRYMANDERING, I'VE GOTTEN CYN A NEW CONSTITUENCY.

THE NERD VOTE IS UP FOR GRABS.

ALL WE HAVE TO DO IS MAKE THEM LOOK COOL BY BEING THE MULTIFACETED DIE IN THEIR DUNGEONMASTER'S CAMPAIGN TO L.A.R.P. THROUGH PROM.

ARE YOU NUTS?

AW, COME ON...

IS MY NAME LIONEL?

DO I *LOOK* LIKE SOMEONE WHO MANUFACTURES *TRAINS*?

YOU KNOW, SUCH GOOD WORK DESERVES A REWARD...

...AND THERE'S ONE NERD WHO HAS YET TO MAKE A LOVE CONNECTION.

BACK OFF, SCREECH, BEFORE I CONNECT MY FOOT TO YOUR ASS.

*UN*BELIEVABLE.

Chapter 3
"Ahh, Cindy B, What's It Gonna Be?"

3

I SWEAR, I TOOK ALL THE GOOD GENES...

HEY, CHECK THIS OUT!

WHAT ARE YOU GOING TO DO WITH THAT, CINDER*SMELLA?*

TURN IT INTO A COACH AND RIDE TO THE DANCE ALL BY YOURSELF?

Gourd engorge.

WOW. THOSE TWO LOOK SO GOOD TOGETHER.

AM I CRAZY, OR IS THIS LIKE SOME KIND OF FAIRY TALE?

THEY REALLY KNOW HOW TO DANCE.

YOU SHOULD TOTALLY VOTE FOR THEM.

HEY, THOSE TWO ARE UP FOR PROM COURT, YOU KNOW.

SERIOUSLY. THE REST OF THE CANDIDATES HAVE CRABS AND STUFF.

CYNTHIA BAILEY AND MARLON SPRINGFIELD.

EX*CUSE* ME?!

OH, LIKE IT'S NEWS TO YOU THAT YOUR LOBSTER TRAP IS INFECTED.

NNNGH.

MOVE IT, *FATTY!*

IT'S PATTY, THANK YOU VERY MUCH.

OH, YEAH? WELL, IF THAT'S WHAT YOUR MIRROR TOLD YOU, THUNDER THIGHS...

...IT LIED!

WHATTAYA SAY, WOLFIE?

YOU READY TO GET WITH THE TOP BITCH AROUND HERE?

HELL TO THE YEAH.

THEN DANCE ME IN THAT DIRECTION, YOU HANDSOME BEAST...

...AND LET'S SHOW THE ROOM...

...WHAT A CLUMSY *OAF* YOU REALLY ARE.

WHAT THE GODDAMN HELL--?!

TOSS

LIFE'S TOO SHORT, GORGEOUS. DON'T STOP DANCING.

SAY WHAT?

AS THEY SAY IN CHECKERS... *KING ME.*

WHY ARE ALL THE GIRLS AT THIS SCHOOL SO BAD AT EUPHEMISMS?

...BUT IT'S TIME TO ANNOUNCE THE ROYAL COURT.

I MEAN, IF YOU DON'T MIND...

FINE BY ME, SOONER I SEE HER LOSE...

SEEING YOUR DISAPPOINTMENT WILL FINALLY GIVE ME A GOOD REASON TO LOOK AT YOUR UGLY FACE.

YOUR PROM KING, BY A WHOPPING MAJORITY, IS...

...MARLON SPRINGFIELD!

AWWW, AND HERE I THOUGHT IT WAS AN HONOR JUST TO BE NOMINATED.

THAT'S A GOOD SIGN.

IS IT POSSIBLE...?

SHARING THIS HONOR WITH MARLON, YOUR PROM QUEEN...

"I WISH THIS BUBBLE WOULD NEVER BURST."

I TOLD YOU, THAT GIRL RUINS EVERYTHING.

I NEVER QUESTIONED YOU. I JUST PLACED TOO MUCH TRUST IN MY FELLOW STUDENTS.

AND WHO DO YOU TRUST NOW?

ONLY YOU, MISTRESS. ONLY YOU.

GOOD..

Chapter 4
"Oh, What's A Matter, Kim?"

4

SIDE NOTE: THIS DRINK IS KNOWN AS THE J&J SPECIAL. SEE BACK OF THE BOOK - DRINKS EDITOR

UM... HI?

POLLY?!

WHAT THE HELL IS GOING ON HERE?

I... I DON'T KNOW.

THERE'S SOMETHING HERE. IN OUR SCHOOL.

AND YOU WOULDN'T KNOW ANYTHING ABOUT THAT "SOMETHING," WOULD YOU?

I SWEAR, I DON'T. IT'S BEEN FOLLOWING US...

IT KIDNAPPED ME!

WHY SHOULD I BELIEVE YOU?

THIS WOULDN'T BE THE FIRST TIME YOU SUMMONED A DEMON ON OUR ASSES.

IT'S A MYSTERY TO ME, I PROMISE.

YOU *LIKE* SPOILING PARTIES. REMEMBER?

I KNOW. BUT NOT THIS TIME.

›hfff‹ FINE.

I'LL PROBABLY COME TO REGRET IT, BUT I BELIEVE YOU.

THANK YOU. YOU DON'T HAVE TO--

STEP OUT OF LINE JUST A LITTLE BIT, AND YOU'LL GO DOWN FASTER THAN DEMI LOVATO ON A PLANE FULL OF COCAINE.

I UNDERSTAND.

EYES OPEN.

YOU SEE ANYTHING FUNNY, YOU TELL ME.

EXCUSE ME, MADAM.

GREETINGS AND SALUTATIONS.

NOT ON YOUR LIFE.

BUT YOU HAVEN'T EVEN HEARD MY QUERY.

YEAH, BUT I ALREADY KNOW IT *IS* QUEER-Y.

THIS IS MOST DISTRESSING.

I WAS LED TO BELIEVE YOU WOULD BE "HOT TO TROT," AS THEY SAY.

WHAT? HOW?

I ASSURE YOU, BY "TROT" I ONLY MEANT HOOFING IT. DANCING, THAT IS.

NO. HOW WERE YOU LED TO BELIEVE I WOULD EVEN TALK TO YOU, MUCH LESS *DANCE*?

THE GIRL WITH THE BLEACHED HAIR TOLD ME.

WOW. THOSE TWO LOOK SO GOOD TOGETHER.

THEY REALLY KNOW HOW TO DANCE.

AM I CRAZY, OR IS THIS LIKE SOME KIND OF FAIRY TALE?

HEY, THOSE TWO ARE UP FOR PROM COURT, YOU KNOW.

YOU SHOULD TOTALLY VOTE FOR THEM.

WORD ON THE STREET IS THAT THE OTHER CANDIDATES HAVE TINY LITTLE WIENERS NESTLED IN THEIR HOO-HAHS.

LIKE PIGS IN A BLANKET.

EX*CUSE* ME?!

WHY? YOU QUIF OR SOMETHING?

I THOUGHT I SMELLED PROCESSED MEAT.

NNNGH.

100

IT'S PRONOUNCED "A JOKE."

LIKE YOUR SEX LIFE.

NOW WATCH AND LEARN, MR. INSANE CLOWN PUSSY.

HEAR ME, MOST PUNISHED SLAVE, FOUL AND UNLIVING.

SUBMIT TO MY POWERS AND ANSWER ME CLEAR.

ARE THESE TWO KNUCKLEBUTTS SABOTAGING THIS PROM?

NEGATORY.

YOU RETARDS ARE OFF THE HOOK.

IF NOT FRED AND LETHAL HERE...

...THEN WHO?

ME? HOW AM I--?

"J"? YOU MEAN JESSE?

IT'S POINTING TO "YES."

I CAN SEE THAT, GLOOMDOOKIE.

GO FLUSH YOURSELF.

CYNTHIA?

ME, JESSE, AND CYNTHIA?

BUT WHY?

SCREW THIS!

EVERY GIRL FOR HERSELF!

ZNK!

ZOK!

YOU GOTTA BE KIDDING--

Chapter 5
"Dance or Die"

5

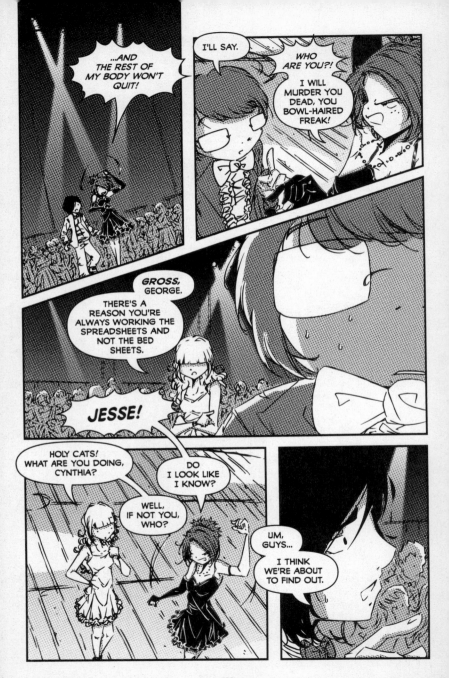

122

PLEASE, MADAM. IF YOU TRULY ARE MISTRESS OF THE DANCE... ...SHOULDN'T THAT COUNT FOR SOMETHING?

WHATEVER DISHONOR THESE YOUNG LADIES BROUGHT ON DANCING WHEN LAST YOU MET...

...SURELY THEY HAVE PAID YOU BACK TEN-FOLD FOR MAKING IT POSSIBLE FOR ALL THESE BOYS TO HAVE THEIR FIRST DANCE AT THIS PROM?

HE HAS A POINT, LAMBADA.

THEY WERE ALL STRIKING OUT BEFORE I GOT INVOLVED.

YOUR *LAPDOG* HERE SPENT THE WHOLE NIGHT INTERRUPTING OTHER PEOPLE, AND SHE LOST PROM QUEEN, TO BOOT.

124

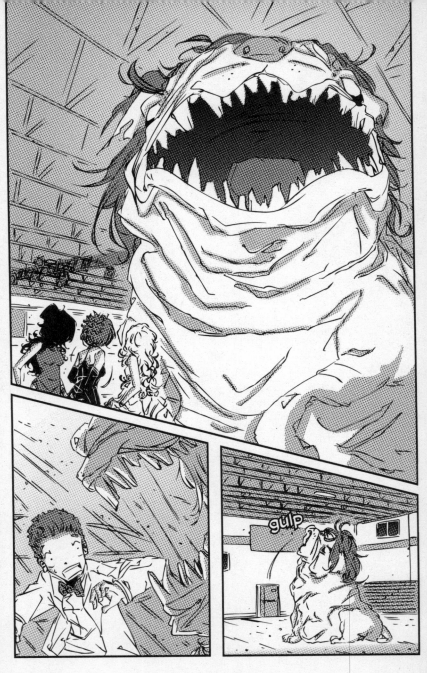

gulp

POP!

WHEEZE!

SPTTR!

POOF!

blink blink

AW, MAN! HOW ARE WE GOING TO GET HOME NOW?

I THINK WE HAVE MORE IMMEDIATE CONCERNS, YOU DOLT.

IF WE DON'T BEAT LAMBADA, WE WON'T NEED A RIDE *ANYWHERE*, MUCH LESS HOME.

LINK UP, LADIES. I NEED YOUR HOCUS POCUS.

Mea gemina...

...no problemo.

Pedis Libero...

SKSH

Erumpo, tremo...

...make me the hero!

KRKK

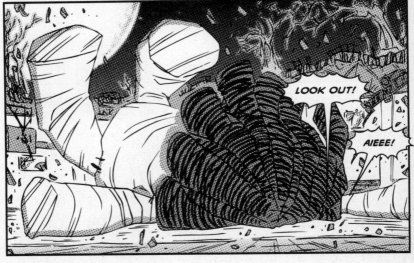

WHOA, REEL IT IN, COMIC BOOK GIRL.

NO WONDER GEORGE WAS SO INTO YOU.

DANCE ON THIS, JERK, AND SEE IF YOU GET A TIP.

HEY, GUYS. DON'T YOU THINK YOU OWE SOMEONE A "THANK YOU"?

WHY? YOU DIDN'T DO ANYTHING.

NOT ME, JESSE...

...POLLY!

GAWD! I *GUESS* SHE DID KIND OF HELP OUT.

KIND OF? SHE KNOCKED OVER THE DEMON AND GAVE YOU YOUR SPELL BOOK.

YOU WERE STUCK IN PLACE, AND KIMMIE WAS ON HER ASS.

AWWW, HE WAS LOOKING AT MY ASS.

HE WUVVED YOU AW AWONG.

144

Epilogue
"It Starts and Ends With You."

OTHER TITLES FROM JAMIE S. RICH, JOËLLE JONES & NICOLAS HITORI DE

SPELL CHECKERS, VOLUME ONE
By Jamie S. Rich, Nicolas Hitori De, Joëlle Jones
152 pages • Digest • B&W
ISBN 978-1-934964-32-3

**SPELL CHECKERS, VOLUME TWO:
SONS OF A PREACHER MAN**
By Jamie S. Rich, Nicolas Hitori De, Joëlle Jones
156 Pages • Digest • B&W
ISBN 978-1-934964-72-9

LOVE THE WAY YOU LOVE: SIDE A
By Jamie S. Rich & Marc Ellerby
200 Pages • Digest • B&W
ISBN 978-1-932664-66-9

LOVE THE WAY YOU LOVE: SIDE B
By Jamie S. Rich & Marc Ellerby
200 Pages • Digest • B&W
ISBN 978-1-932664-95-9

12 REASONS WHY I LOVE HER
By Jamie S. Rich & Joëlle Jones
144 Pages • 6"x9" Trade paperback • B&W
ISBN 978-1-932664-51-5

YOU HAVE KILLED ME
By Jamie S. Rich & Joëlle Jones
192 Pages • Hardcover • B&W
ISBN 978-1-932664-88-1

For more information on these and other fine
Oni Press comic books and graphic novels,
visit www.onipress.com. To find a comic specialty
store in your area, call 1-888-COMICBOOK or
visit www.comicshops.us.

ONI PRESS

www.onipress.com